Children are the Barometers

Registering and reacting to the climate we have made for them

Contents

Dedication

To all the teachers who give their best to their students every day.

Children are the Barometer

Their faces reflect their hearts,
What they do and say mirrors the
Atmosphere in their homes, their
Community, the world we made for them.
In the classroom, if you observe
You can tell not only who has eaten well,
You can tell who has feasted on the love
Of concerned caregivers, or who is suffering
Their mental or physical absence.
The void rends the tender soul
And scars it forever.

Children intuit what their limits are
They touch the walls that confine them
And soon determine that they are
Too high to scale, too thick to penetrate.
And so, they loosen their shoelaces
And discard their belts
Their pants now hang below their waists
And they shuffle along
Like the anti-heroes they
Feel destined to become.

Foreword

Children are the Barometers

These stories are based on actual incidents and places I experienced while I was working as a teacher and as an assistant principal in the Bronx, New York in the 1970's and 1980's. They are composites and not about one child, family or situation. Names of individuals and some places have been altered. Dialogue has been imagined, or reconstructed from memory of words spoken by children in various settings, included here often to illuminate the desperation of a character's unspoken feelings.

I wanted to tell these stories because we read graphic tales about the ex-offender and what he and his family suffer. We seldom hear of the effect of an incarceration on the psyche of his children, what they went through when a parent went missing, how their daily interaction with life was disrupted by the loss of Mom or Dad, how they made their way through adolescence, stumbling, grasping for guideposts no matter how inadequate or detrimental. Or the psychological reasons why child followed parent into a life of crime.

The Drug Wars of the 1970's and 1980's were devastating to the Black and Hispanic communities. Going to prison became a rite of passage for young men; being jobless and having to find a means to life in the underground economy became the norm. More than 60% of the people in prison even now are racial and ethnic minorities. For Black males in their 30's, one in ten is in prison or jail on any given day. 13 year olds have sentences of life imprisonment and nearly 3000 children have been condemned to die in prison.... Prison population has grown from 300,000 to 2.3 million in the last 40 years....These trends had been intensified by the disproportionate impact of disparities in sentencing of those using cocaine or crack cocaine. "Over 90% of those convicted of possessing 5 grams of crack cocaine, a felony offense that carries a 5 year minimum sentence, are Black. This contrasts sharply with penalties for powdered cocaine users, who are predominantly white. Conviction for possessing 5 grams of powdered cocaine is a misdemeanor punishable by less than a year in jail."*

Moreover, communities of color were targeted, and were constantly under surveillance by the police, who at one time, were rewarded financially for quantity of arrests no matter how minor the offense.

Let us look at the lives of these children. How can we protect future students from the perils they faced? How can we find teaching methods that will reach them and let them unleash their creativity, their intelligence, their joy of being alive? As recalcitrant as they seem, they need and want the empathy of adults, if we only knew how to reach into that secret space where the pain is hidden.*

*Michael Tonry, Sentencing Guidelines and their Effects, in the sentencing commission and its guidelines (Andrew von Hirsch, Kay A. Knapp and Michael Tonry, eds, 1987.

Perhaps you might read these stories as springboards for group exchange about action to take against mass incarceration in your community; or have teenagers act out the skits to obtain a deeper understanding of what underlies the behavior of the child in their class who has an incarcerated parent.

I hope that discussion of these stories will accelerate the search for both methods and mentors.

Marietta J. Tanner

March 2016

Students at the Lorraine Hansberry School, 1991. None of these students are depicted in the stories

11

Story 1: Keisha and Malik

I was teaching Language Arts in an intermediate school in the South Bronx in the mid-1970's. In this school, children were placed in classes according to their reading level, but in my class I wanted them all to have a chance at learning the full curriculum, so I would scale down the work to meet their capabilities. If you were reading above grade level and were in the A section, you could earn an A; you had to read A books, you had to read *Cavalcade*, the Scholastic magazine for high achieving students. But if you were on lower grade level in a B or C class, you had simpler books on your reading list, and an easier magazine. Still the work was similar; you had vocabulary, you had to read the factual material and be able to pass the quiz; you had to learn the writing skills, and produce compositions incorporating those skills as a part of the Friday test. These compositions were graded by me, with explanations as to what needed to be done to improve them.

Keisha Jackson was in the C class, she was reading at the 6th grade level in the 8th grade. She was an attentive student. I learned that in grammar school she had been in the top class. But when her father left and they moved to the projects, she began to daydream, became careless about her work, and her grades plummeted. She would never ask a question, her homework was poor, she could not manage the kinds of assignments I gave: Take an inanimate object, make it come alive in a short poem with a rhyme scheme, using a figure of speech. Some kids did funny ingenious things – "Quiet, quiet wall, don't tell all, or I will hit you with a ball." She could do, and would ask for pages, of multiple choice questions as drills; this was the kind of work she was used to. It was the work that was offered in most of the slower classes.

She had trouble applying the rules for writing a paragraph, and writing a poem using rhyme or metaphor was beyond her. I graded her papers accordingly and her mother was furious. I gave her a 75 on her report card, and she warned me, "Miss Tanner, my mother is mad, and she's coming to see you on Open School Night." "Oh that's fine, I really want to talk with her," I said. The kids all looked knowingly: "Her mother don't take no stuff," one boy said. "Good, neither do I," I said. I was truly ill on Open School Night, and even though I came in sniffling the day after, the word was out, "Miss Tanner was chicken; she was scared of Keisha's mother."

You can never let kids know you are afraid, and I really wasn't. I had talked with Keisha's mother before. She was a hard-working, very devout Black woman who put her husband out years before. He had been in prison 3 years

14

allegedly for selling drugs; he used all the family savings to prove his innocence and finally got out of prison.

Cast of "The Heart and the Hand are Ready," a play about the Mississippi Freedom Summer written by the author.

There is a backyard with a grape arbor off Lennox Avenue in Harlem. Every Saturday night, these Jamaican men gathered there, and with lusty voices in unison they would sing Bob Marley's "No Woman, No Cry," and smoke a little Ganja. The men made good money, were licensed refrigeration specialist, plumbers or electricians; they were never out of work as they looked out for each other, and would get jobs for their landsmen. When they came from Jamaica, they already were journeymen or better; the craft unions here, with reluctance, let them in. Not so for the native-born Black men. They were never given apprenticeships. A. Phillip Randolph had railed against the exclusion, to little avail. No question that the native-born Blacks resented these West Indians in the American Federation of Labor, with all the privileges a union card offered. Moreover, the Jamaicans were braggadocios about their abilities and their earnings. I once saw one with a sticker on his car: "We fight poverty, we work," the avowedly racist dig employed white construction workers displayed to ridicule the War on Poverty and the Black jobless families they called "poverty pimps."

It was never clarified: Did the Feds come in that night determined to quickly fill their quota of drug arrests, or did the native-born Black enemies of Mr. Jackson and his Rastas rat on them? Mr. Jackson was in that backyard that Saturday night when the Reggae beat was pulsating; the jerk chicken was cooking on the grill, the scent of marijuana was mixing with the meat and the smoke was rising above the arbor and trees. Even though they regularly paid off the local cops, they were raided; a stash of crack was "discovered," and all were swept up and jailed.

When Mr. Jackson was released, he couldn't get his old job back or find anything steady doing electrical work. Even with his countrymen's help, once the bosses learned he had a record there was nothing even at slave wages. Another woman got in there somehow, and all bets at reconciliation with his wife and family were off. Mr.

Jackson would hang around the apartment building to see his kids; he was on the skids (a classmate said he had become a crack addict). The mother wanted nothing to do with him. She was raising her kids by herself, and she was strict.

I knew Mrs. Jackson's pain, and we had shared what it means to be without a father in the home, as I was a widow. So it was school and church for Keisha. She missed her father, but didn't dare say that around her mother. He had been a jovial dad, who used to read to them and recite poetry, especially Rudyard Kipling's, "If," and other British poems. Maybe that's why she didn't enjoy poetry in school, and didn't smile much. Her life at home was not easy: on her way home after school, Keisha had to pick up her younger siblings; with her latchkey, she opened the door and did not let anyone in, or leave to go out. She started the evening meal, peeling potatoes or making rice as she had been instructed. There were clean up chores, and tasks to do for the younger ones, and while her mother had decreed that they should do their homework when chores were done, they would gather around the television set and watch sexy soap operas.

I told Keisha to ask her mother if I could stop by on Saturday morning around 10 a.m., and I did. Outside the house was a policeman who gruffly said to me, "Where are you going," and I said that I was visiting a student in apartment 5D. "5D," he repeated, "Well ok, but be careful." Word of my visit had gotten out, so there were kids from school gathering; they didn't believe I was going in that building.

One of my other students lived there, who I suspected was already a crack addict, on the same floor. Do I also have the nerve to knock and ask what the problem is with Malik that he isn't coming to school?

I knocked at 5F, and a stout woman set the door ajar, held by a brass chain. "Hello, are you Malik's mother, I am his teacher from the Ida B. Welles School. I'm sorry I don't have an appointment. I'm visiting a student across the hall, but could I ask if he's ok, and when he is coming back to school?" She was so amazed to see me. She wiped her hands on her dress and reached out to shake mine. She invited me in, "Yes he's here," she said, but he's not well. He talks about you a lot and will be glad to see you." The apartment was dark, and there were several couches, on which people were lying. The scent of marijuana or worse was heavy in the air, and it was gray with smoke.

So this is the place where he stole the cross! Malik asked me one day for the gold chain I wore around my neck; he lamented the fact that a man was sleeping and he snatched his cross, but the chain fell in his clothes so he couldn't get it. "What," I said in horror, "Me give you my chain for a stolen cross?" "You steal, don't you, everybody steal," he

18

said. A long lesson for the whole class followed that exchange. The tragedy of his philosophy was perhaps why I spent so much time persuading him to sing, "If I can Help Somebody," for the Martin Luther King Assembly. He told me he sang at his church, and I promised him I would come one Sunday, but I never did. However, he stood up there on the stage and in the clearest, most plaintive tenor voice, and sang the song. No one believed he would do it; the auditorium roared with applause, and I openly wept.

The mother summoned Malik, who entered groggy and disheveled. He smiled sheepishly and immediately began to mumble some excuses as to why he was not in school. "We miss you," I said. "Ms. Smith was hoping you would sing in the chorus this year, she has very few good tenors." He slumped into a chair, and bowed his head. My heart went out to him. I turned to his mother and said, "How did this happen?" She shrugged her shoulders, and said, "What," as if I was not aware of what ailed him. "I'm trying to get him some help." "That's not hard to do," I said, "Are you willing to have him go away for treatment?" "What, I don't want that; they take your kids and you never get them back." She began to get agitated, and I knew it was time to retreat. "If I can help in any way, please get in touch with me; we do miss him at school. Malik, try to come back soon so you won't be left back." He looked up at me as if to say, "You are from another world, woman, I never think of school no more." I asked his mother to come to school and see what arrangements we could make, but she was opening the door with a snarl on her face. I said my goodbyes quickly and went to 5D.

The kids were all about their chores, scrubbing floors, running the vacuum, and gathering up trash. "I am so pleased to see that everyone has household jobs to do," I said. "How are you Mrs. Jackson, I am sorry I was ill and couldn't see you Open School Night, but am so pleased that you agreed to talk with me today."

"I tell you I been meaning to come to see you before; my child has never gotten papers with all those red marks on them and such low grades before," she said. "Are you aware that your child is reading two years below her grade level? She is intelligent and can do better than that." "None of her other teachers give her such bad marks," she countered. "What do they give her, a smiley face; a statement saying good work on a paper they have never read?" Her eyes widened, she realized that was often the case. She accepted this as grading, proof that her daughter was doing ok in school. There are teachers who believe that sloppy teaching is ok for these kids. They believe they have no future in the larger world of science and business, so why bother. Her father is a crack addict, her brother is headed that way, she lives in the crack building down the hall from the biggest crack joint in the neighborhood, so, they take Moynihan's dictum – "give them "benign neglect."

We looked over one of Keisha's compositions, and I called
her into the room. She had understood the lesson, and
learned afterward how to correct her work. But she was
angry at her grade, and refused to do it. And of course,
when her mother sided with her against me, no learning
took place. "It is terrible that your daughter has been given
a second class education," I said," but it is worse if we
accept it and believe it is good enough. I hope you will
begin to fight for the best for your kids; don't let them give
her an A because she is quiet and doesn't cause any
trouble," as I know one teacher said he did." Turning to
Keisha, I said, "What do you want to be when you grow
up?" "A nurse," she said. "On Career Day, talk to a nurse,
see what she says you have to learn to become one, and
begin to study now, because when you get to high school it
will be too late."

There were smiles all around as I left, and I felt I had done
pretty well especially as the kids outside saw that I didn't
have a black eye. The policemen were changing the guard,
getting the count straight about who had visited 5F; I
wondered if they had included me even if they weren't
sure I had made a purchase. I hoped there had not been a
spy inside who might have distorted the count; if so Malik's
mom would have hell to pay.

Story 2: Willie

Spring had returned to Ida B. Wells Intermediate School. National Public Radio was playing the sounds of different birds in various settings such as "Cape Cod Morning," on the radio. I had bought myself a Boom Box and enjoyed taping whatever I found interesting. I considered that I would take my box to my classroom and let the kids listen to the birds. The songs would go nicely with the work we were doing on "Silence," and "The benefits of quiet time for contemplation and mental rejuvenation." The program went over spectacularly; when something happened and the students were upset, they would ask, "Miss Tanner, let's listen to the birds." It was amazing how they tried to identify the songs, and some started going to the Zoological Gardens up the street to the aviary to listen, instead of just run around until they were chased by the guards.

Willie was one of those kids who never visited the zoo, even on free days. He was barred from the Botanical Gardens, as he had been accused of trying to snatch purses as he rode around the drives on his bicycle. He was one of my tougher kids; tall muscular, very dark complexioned, but handsome in his rugged way, with a deep derisive laugh, and a twinkle in his eyes. He didn't know his father. He was a foster child, living with an aunt, who was the single guardian to him and his sibling.

BAMBAATAA, the father of Hip Hop with boom box. He lived in the Bronx River neighborhood, and was the teacher of rap students from the Lorraine Hansberry School.

I had met his mother years ago when my Negro Teacher's Association was enrolling children in Headstart for the first time. I was canvassing Third Avenue and walked the two flights of stairs to visit this young unwed mother and her two sons. Ms. Mason remembered me when she came to school one evening; she told me that Willie was the little boy I had enrolled. She wanted to engage me in conversation, told me that she was clean now, and that she had moved to this neighborhood to be nearer her sister, who, although in an apartment down the hall, shared childrearing with her. Willie was then 12. She was pleased to have a good man in her life at last to help her with her sons; she had been without one since Willie's little brother was born.

But not long after that encounter, she was arrested. This boyfriend she had finally found was a petty dealer. She was unaware that he had stashed some bags high up in her kitchen cabinets. One night the police were sweeping the neighborhood; they knew about the boyfriend, raided her apartment and found the crack. With poor legal advice, and no money for bail, she was separated from her kids, sent to Pawling Correctional Facilities for Women, way upstate. Her sister, who had two children of her own, took Willie and his brother. The two children made possible extra income for her and a larger apartment in the projects. Ms. Mason got ten years for being an accessory to the fact of drug possession.

Willie was a burden to his aunt; he was hard to control. It was rumored that his mother had been on crack when she had him. His aunt soon gave up on him. Willie's adolescence was fraught with anguish – the physical changes were rapid; he was growing a mustache at 13, he was 5'10," broad shouldered and clumsy, and his voice changed before everyone else's. There was no one in the family, no uncle or grandfather, whom he trusted to put his arm around Willie and say, "Son, let's do it this way, or come go with me to the game." So Willie stumbled through the process of becoming a man with crude behaviors he cobbled together on his own. He would cut the lunch line, pushing people aside, and be apologetic about it. He did not realize his own strength, or that his hunger didn't grant him the right to charge ahead of others. He would shove a girl up against the wall who hadn't responded fast enough when he ask her for a pen or paper, frightening her to death.

Willie was not a stellar student; he tried all the tricks with me. He would not conform. He didn't have to do the homework, or keep a notebook or have his textbooks covered. I realized that the thing to do was to get the rest of the class on my side, so they would say, "Willie, for god's sake," we can't go, unless you do..." whatever we had planned for that day. He wanted to be one of the guys more than anything else; he would do outlandish things to make the kids laugh, or be audacious hoping others would follow him.

He was a rapper, and a pretty good one. He would hang out with Olawassimi in the evening at the Bronx River Houses. Olawassimi, with his drumming and musical ability, was developing a rap style later named Hip Hop and had a whole cadre of kids around him. He was a pleasant, disciplined kid who went to Catholic school. I knew him; and although he became head of a well known gang, he waited in the halls to make sure I was ok when I was getting petitions signed and didn't engage in violent behavior. So those who wanted to improve the strength of their rap, kept their minds on the music, didn't smoke, and didn't fight; Olawassimi wasn't about to get put out of the community room where he could work on his creations. Willie wanted to sit in the back of the class and practice his raps; but I made him learn the essentials of poetry, and much to his chagrin he liked it. His raps did sound better with a rhyme scheme and a beat which he learned to measure. When he was especially rattled, he too might ask to listen to the birds.

I could play other things on my boom box such as Christmas Carols to which the students wrote fractured verses like those in *Mad Magazine*. Willie found himself enjoying my English class, doing the spelling and literature, learning how to write paragraphs because it all seemed to have a beneficial effect on his raps. I was pretty smug about how far Willie had progressed; to see him laboring trying to convert his story to a poem was a real accomplishment. I published some of his work in the school newspaper; he was so excited about that, he asked for additional copies and showed them to his aunt with pride.

I was leaving late one afternoon; the schoolyard was deserted, and mine was the only car left on the street. I didn't like to do this, because my tires had been stolen before. One day as a student looked out of the window facing the street, he all of a sudden opened the widow and started yelling at men in the street and for me to hurry, as junkies were removing my tires. By the time the school guard got outside, my car was on boxes. Four men had removed the tires in five minutes. If I had had a Chevrolet or one of the really popular cars for hot-rodding, I might have lost my bumper, headlights, and fenders too. They would sell the parts to corrupt junkyard dealers, who knew the stuff was stolen, for just enough to get their hit. Usually passersby would watch it happen, and say nothing, fearing retaliation.

This day I walked swiftly to my car, as four boys rose out of the courtyard. I was carrying my boom box and a bunch of papers and bags. They were coming toward me, but I thought all was well, as I saw Willie and two other kids I knew in the group. They picked up their pace, and so did I arriving at my car, throwing the box and bags in, slamming and locking the door just as they reached my hood. I blew my horn and shouted for them to watch out, as I was moving. Willie, my student whom I thought I had won over, began to rock my car; two of the kids I knew walked away and stood on the sidewalk to watch. Willie was hyped up now: he pushed and banged on my car, yelling for me to give up the box. He came around the front where I could see him, stretching his arms over the hood. I put my car in reverse; he jumped off or was thrown from the car. Thankfully the street was empty, and I revved my car in reverse for several yards before I was able to clear my attackers and take off.

The next day a repentant Willie met me as I walked into the schoolyard. "Hey Miss Tanner, you know I was only joking yesterday, I wasn't going to steal your box." I curled my lip, "Willie, I am not someone you joke with, I am reporting you immediately to the principal." He was crestfallen; he had gotten into other trouble recently and was known to the police for petty thievery. His love for rapping and wanting to be with Olawassimi and his friends was keeping him away from dealing in marijuana, although I had smelled weed residue on him sometime. He was on the verge of slipping into that hopeless abyss and this kind of infraction might just tilt him over.

Willie was suspended. I didn't want him to be; I asked for an in-school suspension that would offer him regular schoolwork, and a full day of supervision. But it was not to be. Attempting to harm a teacher placed Willie just one step away from being handcuffed and going to the station house. Willie roamed the streets for weeks, became more recalcitrant at home with his aunt, smoked much pot with the older truants, and soon arrived at that place from which few kids recover. He never came back to my classroom; he never came back to our school, and I blamed myself for it. As big as he was, he was only 15 when he was jailed for selling marijuana late one night. He landed in an adult prison, because it was said that he smart-mouthed the cops and struggled with one of them, breaking the cop's arm as he resisted arrest.

Nobody knew anything about Willie as I questioned the kids one day outside the grocery store after I had retired. The paraprofessional I visited told me that she heard he was still in prison, having gotten into fights that got him solitary confinement and extended terms that will keep Willie in prison maybe for the rest of his life.

Story 3: Chino

It is uncanny how kids name their friends and enemies. They read the character of a person and give him a most apropos imprimatur which sticks. On the days he would come to school, a cadre of admirers would proceed him, announcing to me, "Miss Tanner, Chino's here." "Oh really, send him in." I'd say casually.

I was now an assistant principal, but I had known this boy for two years. He really had a photographic memory. He rarely came to school more than three days a week, even from the 6th grade. I had seen both his mother and father. His father was Black and his mother Korean. She spoke very poor English, and always tried to act like she didn't know what I meant when I'd ask if she was aware of what her son was doing. She did not believe in working outside the home, her job was to provide good meals, clean clothes and comfortable surroundings for her husband and children. She had expensive tastes. She wore good woolen suits, tailored to fit her rather squat frame; her hair was long but always tastefully coiled in a shiny bun atop her head. The father was a musician who hung with the cool cats, and was rather dapper. I gathered that he wasn't at home too much, and seemed like a playboy, leaving the rearing of the children to the mother. They had been married since the Korean War, but didn't seem to know each other. When I asked him if he was aware of what his son did after school, he pleaded ignorance too.

31

THE HALLOWEEN SKATE: The author dressed as a slightly graying Pocahontas, with a teacher-chaperone, at the outing for students who were prepared to study.

"He's very ambitious, he's always been the kind of kid who wanted to make a dollar, and that's good, that's good. I'm not gonna interfere in that. He does his school work don't he?"

I had to admit that it was not the grades for which I had summoned them. One of the things I had asked my teachers to do was to see to it that each kid had a buddy who would give him the homework assignments if he was absent; where possible, kids had books to keep at home to which they could refer; they all had to have library cards, a notebook, and all of the accoutrements necessary for their school work by Halloween, it was "trick or treat." If you were certified by your teachers that you were prepared, you got the treat. If not the trick was that you stayed at school while the rest of the 8th grade went to the Halloween Skate.

Chino got the assignments each day; he would interrogate his classmates about what went on, he would read ahead in the textbook, he would appear at school and be the most attentive of students, often asking to clarify something in the lesson. He could scan a page while everyone else was pondering a paragraph and be certain of its content.

Grandmaster Flash was a deejay and rapper, one of the orginals who lived in the West Farms neighborhood.

I asked the parents to help their good student be a great one, but they seemed quite content to maintain things just as they were. I learned from their neighbors that they lived off the money Chino made; he did hustle on the streets both night and day; he was a mule, and had been one since he was nine years old. He never had to write anything down, so no incriminating evidence was ever found on him. Even if a nickel bag was found somewhere in his clothing, he wouldn't go to jail because he was a minor. The police knew him, they knew what he was doing, but they feigned innocence, which was easy because the kid was so small and young. In a show of force, they would sometimes chase him for being out too late, but never take him in –he was too valuable to the whole scheme of things around Southern Boulevard where he usually worked.

I walked outside my office and stood in the corridor as the students trooped pass. There was Chino, dressed in Gucci from head to toe. I called him over. He smiled, and said, "I'm here, Miss Tanner, and I have all of my equipment, Miss Martin will certify me." I know, you have bought your Scholastic magazine and copies for other students too; you have a genuine leather bound notebook, fully prepared with separators, and all your textbooks are covered. Yet, you are not ready."

"What, I followed all the rules, you can't keep me from the Skate." "But you've been absent too much, and those sick excuses just don't fool me; you haven't got asthma and I've seen you on the street at five o'clock when you were supposed to be sick that day. He blew his breath from puffed cheeks, as if to say, "You got me."

I told him to come into my office where I stripped the heavy gold chain from his neck, took the gold three finger and diamond studded pinky rings from his fingers and put them in my safe. I had him remove the leather Gucci coat, but he was still dapper with the signatured pants and pointed shoes. He seemed so relieved to be free of those accoutrements; he was a child again, begging to go out to play; he would prove to me that he would do everything the teachers asked. At lunchtime he crossed the street with an entourage to go to the store. He would buy sodas, and heroes, and chips for all his buddies, and they would sit by the river and eat and laugh and punch each other, running about in friendly horseplay.

The Skate was at a rink a short bus ride away on White Plains Road. For the kids, it was worth all the study and preparation just to get there and roll around the floor on plastic wheels, showing off your glides, putting your arms around the prettiest girls, eating franks until you would fairly burst. Divine Maestro Dee was the deejay. He was the coolest; he would rub the records, making the screeches and blending sounds. And he would rap – rap that new sound, a fast staccato torrent of words would come pouring out. It seemed they all knew what he was talking about. Sometimes they would chime in, shouting out the phrases as they did their cross steps, and smoothly glided up to choose another partner, or just soloed making a statement about their prowess.

Chino was in heaven. He had paid for skates for several of his friends, but never let it touch him, no one was indebted to him. He just wanted everyone to have as much fun as he was having. He came over to the side to ask me why I wasn't skating. I told him that I did not like these new skates. I used to skate on a steel floor, with metal wheels on the skates, and I was pretty good, though it was very noisy. He said it would be easy to show me how to skate on this floor then, but I laughed and said I was too busy chaperoning.

He was so gallant, I wished his parents could have seen him without the burdens of his life of crime. I asked him why he endangered himself hiding in the shadows with cocaine and crack and heaps of cash stuffed in the secret pockets that lined that Gucci coat. Didn't he realize that he had special gifts; that he could be anything he wanted to be? "Why in five years, you could be in college, on your way to becoming....." He raised his hand as if to shut out my voice, and said, "Oh Miss Tanner." He didn't want to hear that kind of talk. Then I said, "What do you want to be in five years? He smiled and with trembling voice he said, "Alive."

That was a prophetic statement. Three years after I retired, I went back to the neighborhood, visiting the projects where some of my students had lived. I stopped in the grocery store where I gave some cash to buy the food that one of my former students had wanted to purchase. She was weeping: she was a day early; the food stamps weren't cashable until the next day. Lurking just beyond the checkout line was a shady looking guy who was furious because she couldn't get the food; he ran up to gather the bags once I paid the bill. The former teacher's aide I had come to visit must have gotten the word out that I was in the neighborhood. When I stepped outside the store, several of my former students had gathered. I asked them about their classmates. Some were unemployed, two had jobs at the Hunts Point market. They mentioned one or two who had done well and were in college; one girl had children already in day care; she took me to the corner of Tremont Avenue and West Farms Road. "Right here, right here," she said, "is where Chino was gunned down. For a long time the blood stain was on the pavement. It's gone now, but we still remember him."

And so do I.

Image of a young man killed on the streets.

Story 4: Marianna

She was new to Ida B. Welles School; she had lived on 163rd Street, but her apartment burned down and the family lost everything. Her father was a small time dealer. He worked well with the few Cubans who pretty much were the kingpins, but somehow he got into a turf war with some Dominicans who were moving in and who he felt were trying to take over. One night they came gunning for him; Mr. Acevedo fired, he maintained, in self-defense, and one of the Dominicans whom he said belonged on Manhattan's upper west side, fell to the pavement dead. The police searched for Mr. Acevedo for a long time; sirens were always blasting around Marianna's apartment, police cars came with flashing lights, and cops, who, like storm troopers, invaded their apartment, scaring the children and interrogating her mother about her husband's whereabouts.

It was during that time that their apartment house was set ablaze by arson; her concerned father eschewing his own safety, crept out of hiding to help them, and was arrested. Now he was at Attica doing murder one; her mother did not expect him to ever come home. Mrs. Acevedo was desperate. Her bachelor brother lived in large apartment in one of the nicer houses. He offered the space to Mrs. Acevedo for herself and the kids.

The Bronx River Project

Marianna loved it there; when the kids turned in their layout of their study space, hers was the largest, with a window, a desk and bookshelves. She was a spunky girl, dark haired with big eyes, slightly plump, but well proportioned. After a while she began to have very pretty clothes, and would talk about going to the theater, and visiting sites that most of the other kids knew nothing about. I was intrigued by her, and asked her if she had considered working toward going to Music and Art High School, as she seemed to have a flair for acting. She said she did, and would like to create a routine for our next show. "Great," I said, "Go talk with Ms. Darden about it, and see what you two come up with."

Ms. Darden was my right hand. I always applied for a grant from the Rudel foundation which gave financial awards to teachers to spend on projects at the City schools. I could hire teachers to work after school on aspects of the work, and buy whatever the kids needed to accomplish the goals. It bothered me that the teacher I wanted often had the least seniority, and some do-nothing would claim the position because he had been efficiently doing nothing for years. But my Principal would work it out for me somehow, and I usually got the effective one. We had an honor society with a classy installation, whose members could be the tutors; the honor roll kids could be mentors, good students could be mediators, and others monitors so that the kids ran the place through their student council . The Environmentalists revamped the riverbank and tested the water with the Bronx Botanical Gardens which was up the street. I got the Planning Board to pay jobless guys to remove debris so we could plant native species on the riverbank.

So many of these men had records; one man about 28, was a very skilled carpenter who built a bench for us and shored up one end of the bank where the soil was eroding. He told me he had never had a full-time job, even though he had graduated from the trade school, Gompers, as a skilled carpenter.

Marianna loved working on the river, and even as her attendance began to fall off, being denied that privilege would make her weep. Ms. Darden and I noticed of late how much she was weeping, and how easily anyone could make her cry. Because she was going through something, I would relax the rules sometimes and let her spend time on the riverbank. She would dig her little plot so carefully, making sure the plants were at the right depth, and following the diagonal pattern. She had by now accepted that there were insects in the soil and they were not roaches. She wanted to be solitary, and the kids (who always knew everything) would leave her alone.

Over the course of the winter, that bright dark eyed little girl who was Marianna became haughty, and less friendly. One day in the hall, some boys were teasing her; I dispersed them and asked her what the matter was. She burst into tears and ran from me. I spoke with the guidance counselor who had noticed nothing, but would contact her mother about the absenteeism. Her teachers, including the music teacher, said her classroom performance was passable, but not as good as it was originally.

I was at the front door during lunch hour when I saw Marianna talking to a tall, handsome Hispanic man, whom I surmised was her uncle. I had met him about a year ago at an evening parent-teacher meeting, when he had come with her mother. But now I didn't like the way he and she were arguing, and the fact that he was touching her, like an annoyed boyfriend. I walked outside, as if surveying the entire scene, he glanced at me, and walked quickly away.

Marianna walked into the grove, and sat on the bench among the fruit trees the environmentalists had planted that were gorgeously in bloom for the first time. I decided not to disturb her, she seemed so melancholic and in need of a moment to confer with nature. But I went upstairs to talk to Ms. Darden who ran the "Just Girls" group. These was mostly Black girls who were behaving wildly, purportedly engaged in sexual acts with a group of Hispanic boys. She was helping them learn social skills, to respect themselves, and stop the fighting with Hispanic girls or joining in the Puerto Rican/ Dominican conflict based on hair and color. Marianna had attended sometimes, but had not been coming of late.

I asked her about Marianna's act; I said I had seen her with a derby hat, and that she looked adorable. Ms. Darden said the act needed a lot of work, but had potential. "Marianna just doesn't have the spunk and sizzle she used to." "Talk with her, will you," I said. Ms. Darden was getting her masters in psychology to become a guidance counselor, and the kids loved her, so I knew she could get to the bottom of this.

How I Met a Worm Face to Face: environmentalists learned
to admire insects.

Mrs. Acevedo, Marianna's mother, came in after much
prodding. She definitely did not want to be there, and
Marianna seemed reluctant to even sit beside her. I told
her how much we thought of Marianna, and that she was a
talented girl who presently seemed to be dealing with

problems out of her control. Mrs. Acevedo said, "Oh no, she is doing fine, aren't you Marianna." Marianna shrugged her shoulders and looked away. "It is obvious that this is a deep problem and you as her mother have got to intervene." She blurted out, "I can't find another place to live, I haven't got the money, and I have three other kids, we will be homeless! Her father is never coming home, he's a parasite, he talks with them and they tell him things, and he calls from prison like a dead man stalking me."

"Do you visit your father," Marianna, I said. "Not much, it's too hard to get there, and he just seems to upset me, he cries all the time I am there, and so do I." Mrs. Acevedo was weeping openly, dabbing her eyes with her handkerchief, "I, I, ah, I don't think I'm going there anymore." Marianne sobbed, "The last time we went, he spitted at her on the glass, he went crazy, the guards had to take him out, but he kept yelling to talk to me, and I was yelling too. It was awful."

The bell rang and I had to supervise the movement in the corridors. "Please wait here, I will be right back." I said. I sent a messenger to bring Ms. Darden to my office, as her first period was free. I waited by the door until she came.

When I returned there was chaos, although the worse seemed to be over. The terrible tale had been told: Mrs. Acevedo had made a pact with her brother that he could

45

sleep with Marianna if the family could have the apartment and he would pay the rent. "I hate him" Marianna was saying, "I hate that hairy face, those clammy hands all over me, do you hear me Mama, I hate him. I don't want his dresses or money, or nothin', I want all of you to leave me alone!" Ms. Acevedo was stammering, "So where are you going, to your beloved father? He has a place for you alright, he has the right to spit at me, but what has he given you for the past three years, just tell me that. How can I take care of four children on a stinking welfare check and the few dollars I make tending bar? You tell me that Miss Hotshot, just tell me that?"

Ms. Darden had to leave, so I sat down with them and said quietly, "If this is so, it is my duty to have you arrested for child abuse, Ms. Acevedo. I am going to call my principal as he is the only one who can handle this case at this point. "

"Oh, you stinking Nigger," she said, "So my children go to foster care and I join my husband in prison. So that's the solution. Satisfied Marianna, you see; now how do you like your situation, putting our business in the street, and now you've got two jailbirds for parents." Marianne looked at her mother with disgust. "So you treated me like dirt, anyway. I'm nothing to you."

"Mrs. Acevedo, let's plan for the children, because you know that sacrificing your daughter was reprehensible. I

46

understand that your husband has parents in the area; with help from the welfare system, can they take care of the children," I asked?

"Their house isn't big enough. I would love to live with Grandma and Poppi. They know, and have tried to get me away before, but they don't have room." Marianna said. "We can find an appropriate apartment, and have your grandparents move in. Your uncle will also get some time, so he won't be bothering you, Marianna. We will see to that."

The guidance counselor and my principal arrived, and after waiting for the classes to change, he escorted the weeping Mrs. Acevedo and Marianna, standing tall and grim-faced, down the stairs to what I am pleased to say was a better life for Marianna.

Story 5: Indigo

They used to call him Indio; it was a while before I knew how the name became *Indigo*, a word not usually found in an 8th grade South Bronx student's vocabulary. I was hoping he would come in today. His customers were bugging me for their jackets, and calls to his home brought no answer.

I will ask the attendance aide to check up on him; it's the middle of the month, his fiery little mother would not storm in demanding her welfare check, which had been withheld because of her son's absenteeism. She would weep and wail about the hours she works, how hard it is to awaken him in the morning. No, he's never there when she gets home after midnight from her 4 to 12 shift; but he always makes it home from school to see her before she leaves for work. They would eat together, she would try to scold him, but it was so difficult. He would be smiling, kissing her, swinging her around – so full of charm, so loving, so much like his father, how could she think that he was lying. When she asked about school, without a blush, he would begin rambling fascinating tales about what he was learning, reading what to her sounded like Castilian Spanish, telling her about Puerto Rico and old Spain. She was so proud of him; so intelligent, so loving. She and I developed a pleasant conspiracy to work together to get her promising boy an education.

The gang was at my door. "What's up, Miss Tanner," You said we could have the clothes by today?" Casually I said, "So what's the worry, I don't want you to get them all messed up before the fashion show, and anyway Alberto hasn't shown today. Have any of you seen him? ""Yeah, last night, he said he'd be in today, and that he was done painting them." "Well, he's mighty late, so we won't be able to count his arrival at this hour as a full school day. I still have your cash; he will want his money, and I will withhold it if he doesn't give me a full day of school work. You can rehearse with Miss Darden without the clothes, she will show you just how you are to model them, and take them off before you begin to dance." They nodded when I asked if they had their white shirts and blue jeans for tomorrow. "I'll be down in a few minutes to see how you're doing."

I frequently had auditorium shows for my 8th graders; they would toe the line to attend or perform. The girls had made outfits in sewing class, which they would model for this pre-Easter show; and they would discuss their budgets, showing how much money they saved. Interspersed with the clothes would be various acts. These boys were break dancers; I worried about their spinning on their heads, but they were good, and they seemed none the worse for wear. Mike was the leader; such a strong guy, a good student, the organizer. He worked in his uncle's car repair business in the evening, got paid, learned responsibility, listened to man talk, and showed it. Respectful, quiet, quite studious, but without the touch of genius, and the aura of celebrity that surrounded Alberto.

Last week, I took yet another commission for Alberto; I could get him to come to school if I held the money for him. The style was those Eisenhower-type jean jackets with the panel in the back – this was his canvass. Alberto made beautiful graffiti-type drawings on them; the kids would die for one. I wish I had gotten one myself; I would have had a work of art to wear.

Graffitied Eisenhower jackets, Courtesy, Museum of the City of New York, The Street as Canvas exhibit

One afternoon as I was leaving school, Alberto ran to me shouting, "Miss Tanner, see that train, see, look." I looked up at the el just clanging into West Farms station; "Watch it as it goes around the corner," he shouted. The other kids were running and pointing too. "Mira, mira, see how *famous* he is!"   There was the elevated train covered windows and all with graffiti. I had to admit it was very ingenious. Spray paint like waves rising from the wheels to the roof, beginning with shades of blue through teal to green, forming a serpent's stylized head and underscored by the tag that read *Indigo*.

Alberto had come to United States at 8 years old, speaking little English. He had been raised by his grandparents, and that's probably why his manners were courtly. They were professionals in Ponce; their son had disappointed them, not because he had left to come to New York, but because he didn't finish college in New York as he had promised. He was so suave, so handsome, so popular that he became a kingpin selling drugs in El Barrio. But when the territory got too small for him, or the Italians got too close, he branched out and moved to the Bronx.

His parents didn't like the woman he chose to love; a stunner, a small boned beautiful person, but without an education, and no family. From the time he was 15 he would go to the other side of town to see her, three years his junior. She hadn't finished high school when she became pregnant, and he married her. He soon left college and took off to New York, and she soon followed, leaving the boy with the grandparents.

From the time Alberto arrived at elementary school, he was a star; he could draw images of people that would amaze.

His drawings were all over the school – he had drawn the principal, and sketched groups of children, sizing them up, shaking his head, biting his lip until he decided what he wanted to reveal about them. When he reached middle school, all the teachers knew he would go to the LaGuardia Music and Art High school, or any of the other select schools he wished to attend. His mother came to school dressed like a princess; diamond rings, a fur coat. Her son was a leader of the pack, quietly standing aside, listening, learning everything; a scholar who would make us proud.

I remember the day everything changed. There was a raid at a club on Southern Boulevard, I saw it on the news, just another drug bust, I thought. They happened every day around the Tremont section or on Willis Avenue, or 149th Street. When will they wipe them all out so our streets will be safe? I had supported our Congressman who had won the election with the slogan "To walk the streets safely...," swearing to get the drugs off the street; every decent citizens looked forward to that. But the next day, there was a cloud over the students; family members were in that club; the police were looking for the bigger boys because they had not gotten their correct take, the kids said. There was a shootout, and Alberto's father took a direct hit.

For days we didn't see him. His delicate mother put on a coat of armor, steeling herself against the new world of low-paying jobs, and run down apartments she now had to face. She appeared at school one morning after being summoned for her son's truancy. The woman who arrived, sans fur coat and jewels, was drab, looking worn and tired. She has tried to get Alberto to come to school, she said. "I know he will, he loves school, but he is missing his father so much," she said, wiping her eyes. Within a few days, the truant officers did bring him in. He received a hero's welcome from his classmates. They knew what Indigo had become – a graffiti artist, risking his life to scale the barbed wire around the train yards; stealing paint from the hardware store, developing his distinctive style, and tagging numerous trains with his name. His paintings always began with blue – and morphed into shades of indigo blended skillfully from the unforgiving plastic gloss.

What is the blues? Did this child even know that music that arose from deep despair in the cotton fields of the South that gave unrelieved sadness its name? The loss of his idol, his father, a loving husband and fabulous provider was profound. Indigo never cried, he threw his tears into his paintings. He was the most daring, the most imaginative artist in the yards; he was *famous* the kids would say, meaning that he was the most prolific, working through the night to get just the right effect, trying to make the indigo blue evolve into lavender then into a bluish-red, then a purple woman's form or some other fantasy shape on many trains. Where was he this day? He needed the money and had promised to come.

I was just getting ready to leave for the day when my principal called. He said that Alberto's mother was in the office, in terrible distress with some jackets for me. I hurried down, fearing the worse, and my fears were confirmed. His mother fell into my arms, handing me the jackets – he worked so hard on these she said. He said he was getting them ready for the fashion show tomorrow. I know the kids will want them. "Where is Indigo?," I blurted out, using the tag. "Last night", she screamed, "he fell between the trains, and one moved, it moved, and he was caught and dragged and wounded and mangled. Ah Dio, ah Dio, my beautiful son is gone."

Story 6: A Garage is Good Enough

The color line in my 1970-80 Bronx school was fierce, openly discussed and argued about among the students. A task for the faculty was to be wise in defusing disputes about the value of light skin or straight hair or any of the trappings of racial superiority that these qualities possessed in the minds of the children. Too often some faculty members supported the concept of white supremacy, and reassured kids that their perception that white was right was correct. Children could be heard proclaiming that the teacher preferred Puerto Rican students who were light or gave better grades to Asian students that were not based on merit. Dominican, Puerto Rican, as well as Black students, especially girls, would get into vicious fights to champion their own complexions or denigrate darker ones, tearing out hair that was long and straight, defacing faces that were too Black, and condemning girls who attempted to be too friendly with their light-complexioned boyfriends.

One very dark complexioned girl whom I will call Marcia, told me that she hated her Black skin. She was shy and retiring because of it, even though she was quite attractive and had beautiful clothes. She could have been a good student, but for her deprecating nature of whatever she did. You could not praise her, whatever she produced was not good enough. She would be snubbed by the Puerto Rican girls whose hair she was always trying to comb and with whom she tried to makes friends.

When her grandmother came to school, I could see the root of the problem. Her grandmother was a light complexioned Black woman with wavy graying hair. Marcia looked somewhat like her, had her slim, shapely body, but was as dark as a Senegalese person, whom the kids said her father was. I never saw her mother, but I understand that she had worked in the sex trade at the Hunts Point Market, and that she was a crack addict, now imprisoned.

It seems that her grandfather was an outstanding businessman, one of the few if only executives in one of the few if only Black companies that had a stall at the Hunts Point Market. There was the Fowler Fowl Company, founded by one Black entrepreneur who made chicken sausages and various kinds of prepared meats that were widely distributed until the 1990's when the founder died, and the new management was not able to keep up the quality or procure the raw product to continue the corporation. Marcia's grandfather was a company executive who was greatly admired for his mathematical skill and ability to handle the affairs of the company, skating through all the obstacles placed before a Black man trying to buy in the wholesale market, trying to get financing, trying to get vehicles and space and to find competent staff. Fowler preferred to hire Black, but was unable to get experienced people since there were so few opportunities for Blacks in industry. His was one of the few corporations that would hire ex-offenders as so many of the Black applicants had been youthful users, picked up in sweeps for marijuana possession and saddled with having to check the ex-felon box on the form. Mr. Fowler was on the board of the Urban League which had job readiness programs throughout the City to train Black young adults in the use of computers and techniques of office management. They finally had a highly competent staff and were one of the few, if only Black food businesses on the New York Stock Exchange during the 1980's.

Marcia did not flaunt any of this background to give herself status. She would cower when some of the Black girls would bully her, seeking money or wanting to "borrow" clothes. To give her a boost, I asked her to be in one of the plays about Martin Luther King's great aunt who had been enslaved. She adamantly refused; she would not take a part as a slave person, even though this was a fine role of an enslaved girl who taught herself to read and was related to our national hero.

There was a club that held meetings on one side of a garage owned by one of the Hispanic kid's uncles. It is claimed that they met after school and invited only Black girls to be entertained there on a mattress which lay on the greasy floor. These were fair-skinned Puerto Rican boys, and some of the Black girls were silly enough to accept the invitation, considering that they were associating with some of the most desirable boys. I would not have known about this had not my right hand teacher, Ms. Darden, overheard a conversation in her math class when some boys were describing how gullible these girls were and joking about the lies they would tell them. Ms. Darden scouted out the site and observed who was entering the den of iniquity one afternoon. She was horrified and decided to go knock on the door, then thought the better of it, as she would have no authority there and would be more effective if she worked on the problem through the school.

She ran the "Just Girls" club which was one of the groups funded by a grant I wrote over the summer which allowed me to hire teachers to develop clubs such as the Environmentalists, the Tutors, the Mentors, The Student Council on an on-going basis, and The Stock Market Club, one year. She was sure some of her girls were visiting the garage and sought them out the next day, asking them to come to a special call meeting, without revealing the reason. I thought we should call it a "Date Wait" program and see if the girls who had not been initiated could postpone sexual intercourse until they were at least 16.

When she saw her math class the next day, she asked two of the boys to remain afterward as she wanted to talk with them. She asked them the nature of the club, and they shyly said it was all about sex. Her relationship with these children was such that they trusted her completely and were very open. She asked them if she could tape their opinions of the girls who visited the sessions. They thought it was a big joke, and readily agreed.

The Black girl removes the white mask.

They spoke about why they thought these girls were vulnerable: they often annoyed them, wanting to play with their hair, making it obvious that they liked their looks, and would do anything to get their attention. They had opinions about their figures, notably that they had larger bottoms than most of the Hispanic girls, so therefore they believe they were extra sexy and eager for intimacy. They recorded how disgusting most of the girls were, because they didn't care what you did or said to them, that they felt they had no self-respect. They said emphatically that they were definitely not in love with them as they often claimed at the session.

On the day Ms. Darden gathered the girls, she had a light repass, and had them meet at her house, so that they would be comfortable and relaxed. Marcia was among them. She had not actually been seen going into the garage, but was a regular at "Just Girls" so was able to attend. Ms. Darden began by casually speaking about color and hair and just how they regarded their appearance. She had nail polish and grooming instruments, so the girls were talking among themselves as they filed and polished each other's nails. She listened and interjected provocative words and ideas as she moved among the group. She was appalled at the low self-esteem most of the girls had, how everyone who was light, no matter how ugly, was better looking. Some of them were beginning to wear expensive extensions in their hair to compete, they thought, more favorably with the long blowing hair some of the Hispanic girls had. This was Dr. Kenneth Clarke's Black and white doll choice experiment, that was instrumental in the 1954 Brown vs Board of Education decision, in action.

One of the things that struck her was Marcia's comment when they got around to talking about motherhood and how they must protect themselves from disease if they wanted to be good mothers someday. This retiring soft spoken young girl said in a voice more loudly and with more confident resolve than anyone had ever heard, "One thing is sure, I am not going to have any Black children!" "Well, what kind are you going to have," the girls all laughed, "You're plenty Black." Marcia retreated to a corner, and was silent for the rest of the afternoon.

Finally, Ms. Darden ask the girls if they knew any of the boys in the garage club. After looking around sheepishly, two girls said they knew one. "Is he your boyfriend," Ms. Darden asked. "No, but he said he likes me," a girl named Naomi said. With much emotion and angry gestures Beryl said, "I don't think so, I don't think so, you think so, but he is not interested in you." "What makes you think he's interested in you," Naomi said. "He told me he likes me, in fact he asked me to go with him," Beryl said, with confidence. Then Ms. Darden said, "Did you agree?" to which the girl nodded her head, "Yes." "And what were the terms of this agreement?" Ms. Darden asked. "Is he going to take you out to the movies, or the baseball games? Is he going to parade you around the school in front of all his friends declaring that you are his new girlfriend?" "Has anybody here seen them together sitting under the apple trees having lunch? Has anybody here seen them on a date at the skating rink?"

There was an undercurrent of shock; no one was laughing. These girls had never thought of what it meant to go on a date. Unfortunately, after further discussion it was obvious that they thought they had no other assets except their sexuality. Where were the mothers of these children? What had their fathers told them of their value as human beings? I found out later that of the nine girls in the group, there was only one child who lived with her father and mother; two had fathers who were incarcerated, two were foster children, and amazingly, four of them were being reared by their grandparents.

Ms. Darden passed out some booklets on dating that talked about associating with groups of boys when you are a young teen, not going steady, avoiding intimacy and learning how to protect yourself. Some of the girls had seen the pamphlet before and laughed at it, calling it "corny." Ms. Darden asked them to take another look at it and learn what it means to date. "There's a difference," she said, "between being a sexual object and forming a relationship with a boy; or being a slut who boys make fun of and being a girl whose company he cherishes." Then she asked, "What do you think those boys at the garage think of you?" There was a chorus, from girls she thought had never been there as well as the two who had admitted they were invitees. "They like us, they give us sodas and they...."

"Please," Ms. Darden said with exasperation, "Don't accept money or "things" from men who are just trying to use you. Be able to say, "No." You don't want their junk, you can get sodas and heroes for yourself or do without. Please girls."

She was emotionally wrung out by this time, she had opened a can of worms she had not thought was this tragic. She went over to her tape player, then turned to the group and said gravely, "I want you to hear what those boys think of you; I want you to listen carefully; I want you to take stock of what you are doing to your reputation, your life, by throwing your pride away for something as useless as a sexual encounter with a good looking boy who thinks you are trash." She played the tape, to complete silence, then gasps, then tears. The boys said how disgusting these girls were; in crude terms they explained what they had allowed them to do; they said that the girls didn't ask anything of them, were laughing and seemed grateful for their attention. They didn't even walk them home at the end of the afternoon, and indeed they wouldn't take them anywhere.

I had listened to the tape the minute Ms. Darden got it and provided the funds for the afternoon outing. The next day I wanted to know the results of the soiree, and whether it would have any lasting effect. I had the clubhouse closed after a meeting with the landlord uncle, and disclosure of the rumors about what went on there. The girls continued to come to the "Just Girls" sessions with greater enthusiasm as they went on shopping trips, visited a grooming workshop, saw more films on dating, and learned various things about finding a career and making good use of their talents.

I wanted to find out more about these homes; where were the fathers and mothers, and what was preventing them from educating their young girls about the birds and the bees? I called the parents together for a session with me and Ms. Darden at the school. Most of them came. It was interesting how many of the homes had been devastated by drugs. The two girls who were in foster care were twins whose mother was serving twenty-five years to life for second degree murder. She and their father had a crack house, where they were caught cooking the substance by a rival who tried to shake them down; they shot him, and were sentenced to Peekskill Correctional facility.

Beryl, like Marcia, never knew her father. Beryl's mother had gotten pregnant by one of the boys selling drugs on the block and given birth. The boy has since disappeared, to which her grandparents said, "Good riddance," and took custody of the child. Her mother finished high school and is now working.

Marcia's father was said to be a fork lift driver at the Hunts Point Market; a tall, slim, muscular man with aquiline features who dominated Marcia's attractive young mother

66

and made her a drug addict. She used to hang around James Madison High school with a fast gang after school, and started going to the Market to get free marijuana cigarettes with the group. Soon she was taking stronger drugs supplied by this Senegalese man who would meet her at a trailer site. Her father was helpless to extricate her from this handsome exotic Black man, despite law suits and raids. She left her comfortable home for her supplier, became pregnant by him and finally ended up in New Bedford Prison for women.

Naomi's grandmother was rearing her, and not doing a very good job of it, as Naomi was not easy to handle. She was seven years old when her grandmother took custody and had witnessed a lot of mayhem and illegal behavior. Her parents were killed in a drive by shooting; victims of a drug turf war it is said.

The other girl who lived with her grandmother was the child of a teenage mother who was being reared as if the mother was her sister; other siblings in the home were unwed parents, and a legacy of illegitimate births seemed to be the norm. No father figure was present.

The two girls whose fathers were imprisoned lived in the projects; their mothers worked long hours and were able to give little guidance at home —only one of the mothers attended the meeting. The one who came, Mrs. Logan, said that both fathers were imprisoned for possession and got extraordinarily long sentences which they considered unfair. She had moved from the south without her husband and was rearing the girl on her own. The father had come north, but was of no account, was on drugs and has not supported his child. Mrs. Logan said, the other woman's husband had been chronically unemployed. Once imprisoned he was not able to find work. "So he left her with three children to raise alone. Now he's been picked up again."

The one girl who lived with her parents had broken the code of honor which both parents purported to be their standard. Mother and father were shocked that their daughter felt the way the other girls did, and threatened to take her out of the school. I told them that there was no hiding place; that's why the complexities of race and society are a community problem which we must all work to solve.

I had gotten a short film from the Schomburg Library for Black Culture about the noble history of Black people, about our roots in Africa, about how we had overcome great hardship to arrive at this place, and what Malcomb X said about our obligation and the necessity for us to honor our blackness. The one male who was there didn't appreciate being called Black; it was amazing that he felt that way in the 1980's when so much had been learned about Black being beautiful; Nina Simone had sung about it,

Martin Luther King had prayed about it, and here this man wanted to be called "colored," as "I am not Black," he said. "Neither are white people white, nor the Chinese people yellow, nor native Americans red," I said, "Those colors are used to designate a racial group, and we accept that being Black differentiates us from brown people, like the Indonesians or Mexicans. Whether you want to acknowledge it or not, your child is being designated as Black, and she must be proud of who she is or else she will not value herself." He talked about getting away from this community, "Too much drugs; too many people selling that crack on every corner." "True, but let's focus on what's going on in the home, that is where the foundation is, that is your fortress against all that is happening outside. Some very fine kids have been raised in this neighborhood who were never sucked into the drug scene. It's the kids who need a crutch who become addicts; they are searching for something to lean on, someone to turn to when there is a problem. When there is no parent, the fixer finds them."

Marcia's grandmother spoke up, "I want to tell you about my daughter. We thought we were doing everything right, we sent her to a private school. Kids got the impression that she thought she was better than those other girls who lived down the block. After all, she lived in one of the best houses in the neighborhood, she was light complexioned and had long hair, and she talked of going to college and being somebody. We gave her things, which she would often give away, because she wanted to fit into the group; she wanted to be popular. My husband worked all the time, and I just believed everything she told me: that she was in a conversational Spanish club at James Madison High after school. That's how she started smoking pot. We have got to spend more time with our kids and be close to them so they will talk with us. Now I hardly know who she is when I visit her in prison. I don't see any remorse in her and wonder what she will do when she comes out. I'm trying to be close to my granddaughter, but it seems I am making the same mistakes," she sobbed.

Ms. Darden and I continued the conversation and provided avenues for enlightenment for the girls and their parents. Maybe it was the power of the media, with its emphasis on white beauty, its Black stars seeking to emulate them, except in more revealing costumes and songs with more vulgar lyrics. Our children subliminally received constant urging to be something other than who they were, to reach a standard of beauty that was unobtainable. That standard has been challenged by the Black is beautiful movement. Yet the heroines in Spike Lee's movies remain light complexioned with Caucasian hair; the dark complexioned woman with the short Afro is the villain or the unpopular clownish girl. This thinking has to change, and our girls must see African and women of African descent taking the lead in finance and government and being married to handsome men of many races. But we hadn't arrived there yet, and the scramble was on, as these girls saw it, for them to improve their status by association with a "whitish" desirable guy, even if he didn't desire them.

Mrs. Logan talked the problem over with her imprisoned husband when she visited him. She showed me the letter he wrote to his daughter. The child read and re-read the letter, asking her mother to explain some of the history about the plight of sexually exploited Black enslaved women. The letter brought them to the point of conversation about intimacy for the first time.

Marcia dropped out of school. The kids told me that she was pregnant. I was dumbstruck, and called her grandmother. She verified the rumor. Not only Marcia but two other girls who were in that group were also pregnant. "My god," I said, "How did this happen." She wasn't sure and couldn't get much information from Marcia. I told Ms. Darden about the situation and asked her to speak with her garage club boys to see if they knew any of the facts. They were very reluctant to talk about this situation, but after much prodding and some detective work, Ms. Darden found the answer. A member of the former garage club was the child of an incarcerated father. His mother became ill, was sinking deeper into depression and had to be hospitalized. She went away for two weeks to a clinic and left her son at home with an older brother who was working most of the time. These three girls visited this young man at his home during those weeks and he had managed to impregnate all of them. If you have ever felt thoroughly defeated, you know what Ms. Darden and I suffered that afternoon. Then we said to ourselves, we were 2/3rds successful as the other six girls were doing fine; their parents were in touch with us, and they were dancing at the afternoon parties with Black boys and not caring whether the Puerto Rican boys ask them for a dance or not. They swore they were practicing our Date-Wait program.

It was the last week of school when I was putting away my supplies and locking my closets as school closed for the summer. A few students were helping me. One of the girls ran in very excited. "Miss Tanner," she said, "Marcia is here." I stepped down from my stool, and beheld a smiling Marcia, 14 years old with a beautiful little baby boy, all dressed in blue in her arms. "Hello, Miss Tanner, isn't he cute, this is my baby." Marcia, I said, how are you going to take care of a baby, you haven't even finished junior high school?" "Oh," Miss Tanner, "My grandmother is helping me. Isn't he cute? He's got curly hair." She proudly took off the baby's hat to show me; indeed he was golden brown with huge dark eyes and ringlets framing his face. "He is adorable," I said, "But Marcia, you have got to make plans to go back to school and get an education so you can take care of him. Who's the father, and is he paying child-support?" She named the boy, and then said, "No, my grandmother is helping me." I asked her if she thought this was a burden for her grandmother who had to take care of a grandchild and now a great grandchild. She started crying, and said her grandfather wasn't very nice to her anymore. She was hoping to get a welfare check to help her take care of the child, but she is too young and has to have a guardian, so she has to live with them.

The situation was similar for the two other girls; very angry mothers, very desperate mothers, barely able to care for their own children and now saddled with a grandchild. A satellite school was established in the district to permit the girls to bring their babies each morning, learn mothering, nurse their young, and continue their education. I made sure the three of them were enrolled and monitored their attendance. They did not seem remorseful; indeed, two were defiant often complaining about the putative father wanting him to take some interest in their child, berating their mothers for not helping more with child care. The absence of their own fathers was palpable. How different might they have been had their fathers shown them the depth and devotion of paternal Black love, holding them close and saying that he valued them just as they were dark complexioned with kinky hair. If we ever wondered what drug addiction and massive drug arrests have done to the family, the girls in the Maternity School were classic examples of impaired development, demonstrating by their behavior as adolescents the need to understand their own sexuality and how it relates to the male of the species.

A Message to a Graduating Class

The Will to Prepare

Here I am in my favorite place, surrounded by the happy faces of students. Most of these became LandaHand Leaders – students who developed their leadership skills by helping others. And then, the idea of reaching out to others became the theme of this year's class. What a way to go – our students deciding to take personal responsibility for the well-being of just one other person! Such a movement could uplift our school, our city, our nation.

Everyone wants to succeed. Teachers point the way, but it is so much easier to learn when our peers are rooting for us. We hope we have offered you a place, not only where you could stumble, fall, get up and start over, but where you also could PREPARE yourself for citizenship by taking a neighbor's hand.

As we watched the NYC Marathon in October, we saw an African win for the second consecutive year. A man who used to run five miles to his school every day, over the roughest terrain, in high altitudes, beat out others trained in the finest gymnasia in the world. Of his struggles, he said, "The will to win means nothing without the will to prepare."

We hope we have helped you, and that you have helped others, PREPARE for the tasks that lie ahead. The terrain will be rough – a depressed economy will strip away many of the cushions your predecessors enjoyed in high school and beyond. But you have weathered rough terrain at Hansberry – You know the way. Continue to PREPARE yourself, and earn the right to win.

- Marietta J. Tanner, June 1991

Dramatizing the Issues: 3 Skits on Mass Incarceration

Just Promise

(skit for Children are the Barometers)

- At a pay phone in a prison:

Darrell: Hi Baby, how you, whose that talkin' in the background, where are the kids? You coming up here next week?

Cynthia: Wait a minute, cool it, no body's here, that's the television. I'll turn it off, I never know when you're going to call so I don't have everything nice a quiet just for you.

Darrell: It's hard to get a phone, and harder to get the $7.00 to talk for just a few minutes – so, are you coming up next week?

Cynthia: Now that's hard, to get the money to come up there- why you have to go way up to Peekskill; I'm not bringing the baby.

Darrell: What, I want to see him, I only seen my son one time. I been waitin' and workin' for next weekend for three months; guards and everybody else been kicking my ass, and I been takin' it; one little misstep and it would take another three months before we could have a conjugal; please, bring him.

Cynthia: You just expect so much; Getting up before day to catch that bus, lugging that food and the kids and the clothes, I'm tired of the whole mess; you just try to keep things going in this project: cleaning, cooking, washing at the laundromat where somebody always stealing your stuff, scared to take the kids out, trying to make it on food stamps and the few bucks from SSI, and then, and then visiting you, and getting another baby to add to my burden, and you just waitin' behind bars for me to ride 90 miles on that hot bus – like you think I'm going to Hawaii-- to see you.

Darrell: Look, Babe, they are workin' with the laws, now; they releasin' guys that got picked up durin' the drug sweeps, I been workin' on my case. A group called the "Sentencing Project" was up here with some people from ACLU; they are gettin' guys like me sprung; I may be home by next year.

Cynthia: Next year! 15 years in jail – I am so tired - your daughters are near grown, and now we have this baby. Lucky me, you became such a good jailbird that you could have sleepovers with your wife, and now, you have a son, and I have to start all over again with diapers, etc, etc. with no-one to help me. Even if you come home, where you gonna work? – We'd have to move out of the projects, no one with a drug record can live here.   I am so tired! (Sobbing).

Operator: Two minutes, sir.

Darrell: Listen Babe, just come next week, we'll talk it all over. I swear, I'm talkin' with those ACLU guys; they not

79

gonna let the cops pick up guys off the street and put a nickel bag of stuff on them and throw them in in jail, and throw away the key like they did me. I been studyin' here, I been tryin' to learn a trade, I can read now, I can make a livin' for us.

Operator: Time is up sir.

Darrell: Cyn, Babe, just come up next week, promise, just promise.

Marianna

A prisoner enters from the left with a guard:

Guard: Now listen Acevado, hear me well, if you start that screaming and cursing like you did last time, forget about having any more visitation rights.

Acevado: Aw man, if you knew my troubles; never seeing your sons, your daughter, can't protect your kids, man it just kills me.

Guard: So sorry, you should have thought about all that before you shot the guy.

Acevado: It was self-defense, I swear, if I coulda had a decent lawyer, I wouldn't a spent a night in jail.

Guard: Yeh, yeh that's what they all say.

Acevado: He was comin' after me, gun drawn, shootin all around me, whatdoya think....

Guard: And you all was dealing drugs, so ok. I'll take off the cuffs, just sit there quietly and wait for your wife and daughter – she's 13, right, she can see you, but no cursing, I'll be waiting right outside, any trouble, and all bets are off.

Acevado paces back and forth, then sits down waiting by the window. –A woman and girl enter from the right.

Mrs. Acevado: You go and talk with him, I'll just sit here; he doesn't want to see me.

Marianna: (*running toward the window*) Poppi, Poppi (*she places her hands on the glass, he reaches up puts his hands*

82

against hers, then his cheek, she presses her mouth to the glass to kiss his cheek. Oh, Poppi, I miss you so much, (*she sobs.*)

Acevado: Que bonita, Que bonita my little girl getting ready for your Quincenara, soon you will be a woman, and I am missing all the beautiful days. Marianna, you are my treasure.

Marianna: Quincenara – (sneers) that's for girls who are virgins, not people like me, and you know it Poppi.

Acevado: (*shakes his head, stares*) No, no Bebe, no no, don't say it, I can't bear it, say it didn't happen. I sit here and go over the night I killed that Dominican dog; I relive the fire that could have killed you and your brothers, I see the blazing apartment, I couldn't stay hidden, I had to come to see if you were all right, I had to.

Marianna: Oh, Poppi, I remember, you tried to help us, that was the last time I ever saw you... outside - ever touched you (*puts her face against the glass again.*)

Acevado: Tell me about school, Bebe, are you still acting in the plays, are you still singing, are you still my star student?

Marianna: Oh, Poppi, I try, I try, but I can't study, I hate to go home, I just hate him so much. I don't want his clothes, I don't want nothing from him. I wish we could go back to our old apartment, just you, the kids and Mamma, just like it used to be.

Acevado: (*Visibly shaken*) Where is she – where is that bitch who I used to call wife, where is she?

Marianna: Poppi, no, no, I'm sorry I said it, but it's so hard. I was hoping you could help me get away…. Why can't I go live with gran gran and poppa? *(cries) (Walks to the right, to summon her mother)*

Acevado: Tell her to come here, I gotta see her, I will calm down. *(Walks away from the window, rocks back and forth)*

Mrs. Acevado: Miguel, what is it? Don't start screaming at me. Tell me that it woulda been ok to be homeless, to let my kids starve while you sit up here in the comfort of this jail. Tell me what a beast I am to move in with my brother, until I can get on my feet. Tell me how I was to support a family of four with no husband, no apartment, no furniture, no food and no job.

Acevado: What about welfare – decent women manage, raise their children with dignity, why couldn't you do that until I can work out something?

Mrs. Acevado: You, work out what, nothing, nothing, Hah, tell me what magnificent plans you have been talking about with Marianna. Whenever we come, you fill her up with dreams, and she becomes impossible. She promised to behave if she could see you again, and I fell for it. Yes, I would fall for any straw of hope so I can manage this horrible life you have given me.

Mr. Acevado: Other women make it, what about living in the projects, you too proud for that?

Mrs Acevado: Oh what wonderful solutions you have; you want me to live worse than a peon, scrounge around and see how wonderful it is to live on food stamps, in roach infested, rat-infested, crime ridden projects, uh, huh, you want me to suffer, become the scum of the earth.

Mr. Acevado: (sneering) You are the scum of the earth. You sacrificed your beautiful daughter – sold my daughter to that slime of a brother of yours for an apartment and a few bucks a week. What's more despicable than that? Tell me, tell me?

Mrs. Acevado: Oh, Miguel, she will be all right, this kind of thing has happened to women for centuries – it was custom in some societies, the privilege of the lord of the manner, some of us, desperate people like us, had to live it, those women had to survive. (Crying)

Marianna: Mamma, You think it's ok, Mamma, but it's me who has to sleep with him, feel his clammy hands, his hairy face; everybody knows about it, all the kids at school, it's just awful.

Mr. Acevado: (*Screaming*) She is a witch, she sold my daughter to her stinking brother, and thinks its ok, (*bangs on the window, Screams.*) If I could get my hands on you, you bitch...

Guard: Ok, Acevado, that's it, times over, (*2 guards rush in and handcuff Mr. Acevado*)

Marianna: Poppi, Poppi, when will I see you again? Don't go Poppi, Don't go, I have something to tell you, Poppi....

(Mother pulls girl off to the right, both are sobbing)
(Father's screams can be heard).

85

The Lifer

(A prisoner, behind a slotted door with a barred window, is screaming as two guards and a physician enter the scene.)

Guard 1: We're going to straight jacket him; there's no other way. Just wait until you see him – bloodied from banging on the walls, big holes everywhere, his mattress torn up, excrement all over the floor, he's just impossible.

Physician: Yes, I know, however we can get him out to be hospitalized we must do it. He's going to kill himself, and he's so young. I can't imagine how we let things get this way.

Guards (Look at each other in disbelief) What?

Physician: When you finally calm him down and he starts to talk about himself, he's like the teenager who came here ten years ago, just for being with a gang of ruffians, breaking store windows, stealing merchandise, and now he's a lifer – without the possibility of parole. (*She shrugs and turns away*)

Guard 2: (*Aside to Guard 1*) Oh, she is a softy! She didn't mention, they beat up that Korean guy pretty bad, too. But, she doesn't have to deal with him; I have known him for years. When we go in that cell, step carefully. He can make a shiv out of anything.

Guard 1: He was once among the trusties. How about that day he got mad – mad because he didn't like the spaghetti sauce, started throwing plates around, and we took him out. Somehow, he concealed a fork on himself in the chaos, and made himself a knife. You remember that, Chief?

Jose: (*overhearing and sneering*) Hah, crazy Jose, just didn't like the sauce, heh. You shits eat that spaghetti sauce, see how you like it.

(The warden walks up.)

Warden: I do indeed, he was slashing everything and everybody who came near him. Let's see if we can talk with him, get him to put his hands in the slot. Come over here with the cuffs.

Jose: Yeah, (*screams*) Yeah, that bastard spit in my spaghetti; yeah, some bastard was always messin' with me, you know it, you know it. *(Yells, howling like an animal)*

Guard 1: Okay, Jose, "siente se," they understand now, they're going to help.

 Jose: Help, ha, ha. Ya'll just let 'em do what they wanted to a curly haired, blue-eyed kid like me; Ya'll didn't stop none of them passin' me around like a whore, did you? I'd kill that bastard again, do you hear me; I'd kill him again right now if I could see him.

Guard 2: Com'on, com'on, put your hands up here. It's over, he's gone; he won't bother you no more.

Jose: Gone, heh. I vomit when I think of him, spitting in my food. Eat it, eat it, you belong to me, eat my spit, you're mine, eat it. (*Screaming*).

Warden: He will go on like that for hours; the psychiatrist told us years ago that he was hallucinating; but he just sat quietly singing to himself; he wasn't a problem.

Guard 1: Why didn't they send him to a juvenile prison, he was such a puny little kid when he came; probably he wouldn't have gone off this way?

Guard 2. He was 15; the grocer who was the victim was permanently crippled. Definitely he's off his rocker now.

Jose: (*being bundled in straight jacket, and placed in a wheel chair*). (*Looking around wildly*) Crazy Jose, ha, ha. Took me years to get him, years watchin' and waitin"til I could stick his butt. All his buddies are out here. (*Calling out to the locked cells*) Hello, Hello, you sons of bitches, I know you're watchin'. All you bastards that used to hold me down, laughin' and feelin' all over me. I'll kill you too. I'll kill you too. All of you are going to hell. (*Screaming*)

Physician: What a pity, all that time in solitary didn't help him. So young, too young to have no one to talk with for months, days, years; we know what it does to people, how the mind deteriorates; now he's got murder one on his record. He will never get out.

Postlude

There is a reason why the acceptance of prison as a rite of passage became ingrained in the ethos of poor Black teenagers. "Scholars" seized upon the aberration that most prisoners were Black and concluded that it was because of the Black criminal mind. In the 1950's, several studies proclaimed that African Americans had a proclivity to perform unlawful acts. The Black elite felt justified in shunning the incarcerated and ex-offender as having disgraced the race by succumbing to the stereotypical image of Blacks as petty thieves and criminals.

From our lives as an enslaved people, our survival might have depended upon pilfering from the enslavers, a kind of rebellion against hunger and deprivation. We internalized the stereotype of Black lawlessness, made many self-effacing jokes about it, and accepted the characterization as real. It was a mark of oppression, a scar indicating second-class status and intellectual inferiority. When the Civil War ended, the liberated slaves were uneducated, penniless, homeless, and landless; few if any got the forty acres and a mule. Moreover, "states passed discriminatory laws to arrest and imprison large numbers of Black people, then lease the prisoners to private individuals and corporations (See Bessemer Steel, Alabama) in a system of convict leasing that resulted in dangerous conditions, abuse and death...."** Thousands were forced into a brutal system that historians called "worse than slavery."****

The 13th Amendment of 1865 did not end slavery. It made "slavery and involuntary servitude <u>unconstitutional except as punishment for a crime</u>. The southern labor market bereft of slave labor, depended on the criminal justice system to become the primary means of continuing involuntary servitude of African Americans."** In most states, the incarcerated were considered property of the state until recently; prisoners today are being exploited, producing products for corporations at far below the minimum wage. Moreover, once the person is released, second class citizenship endures. The exonerated is subject to "legal discrimination in every aspect of citizenship: housing, voting, education and public benefits forming a racial caste system."*** With so many of our fellow citizens having been victims of unjust imprisonment under the "War on Drugs," with our communities having suffered the absence of fathers, husbands and sons, with young Black men and women today being shot in questionable encounters with the police, with joblessness being a consequence of lost productive years and their criminal activity correlating with inadequate schooling, the entire community must look for solutions, as none of us can escape the effects of the scourge.

Nineteenth century Immigrants from Europe, Jewish death camp survivors from World War II, refugees from horrible conditions and war in the Middle East and Central and South America got and are now getting Federal help with housing, education, health care and business startups; none of this largesse was available for the Blacks who were forced to sharecrop on the old plantations or migrated north after the Civil War and in the post, World War I Great Migration. Nor were there reparations for the 300 plus years their labor was stolen and its benefits used to enrich the corporations of our nation.

Our children are impacted by this history even as they deny any connection to slavery. They look for escape; they hope for luck to remove them from their plight; they want instant gratification and don't believe in the long-term process involving study. In fact, they question their ability to learn and what the benefits of an education might be, having seen the results of so many doors being slammed shut from their ancestors. On their small shoulders they carry the burden of a history replete with hopelessness and of labor without reward.

In my farewell statement to my students, "The Will to Prepare," I sought to let my students know how capable they were; to think about what could be accomplished with perseverance, and that their future was full of possibilities. I could only say this because I was involved in the struggle to end mass incarceration and active politically and socially to make a more just and egalitarian world for them.

If we become engaged in that effort and tell them the story, if we help them understand what has been imposed upon them, and help them remove the shackles, we can do much to halt the escape to substance abuse, we can stop the reliance on the "quick fix" of a drug or criminal act, and perhaps we can build our communities strong with our young men and women standing tall.

Marietta Jones Tanner, March 2016

**Stevenson, Bryan, "Just Mercy;" Equal Justice Initiative, A History of Social Injustice, Prison Labor and the 13th Amendment, Montgomery Alabama, 2/26/16.

***Alexander, Michelle, "The New Jim Crow, Mass Incarceration in the age of colorblindness," The New Press, 2010, ISBN#978-1-59558-643-8

****Oshinsky, David M., "Worse than Slavery, Parchman Farm and the Ordeal of Jim Crow Justice," Free Press, 1997. ISBN#0684830957

Picture credits

Graffiti Bombed Trains, Martha Cooper, Art Vs Transport. S.B. 1982, Museum of the City of New York, City as Canvas Exhibit.(Cover)

Babbaataa with boombox, race cars-and-weed-jarsTumblr.com.

Grandmaster Flash - All Music - Allmusic.com, Rap to turntablisdm, 1/2000 (Pinterest) (Chino)

Black Girl removes White Mask - Art Ideas, Harmony Finearts/art.ideas (Pinterest) (A garage is good enough)

Rest in Piece Memorial, Early NY Subway Art, Graffiti Memorial, the Bronx Lens, Pinterest, Parkchester. (Chino)

Graffiti Jackets, courtesy Museum of the City of New York, City as Canvass exhibition (Indigo)

Dondi spray painting a train, Martha Cooper, Art vs Transport, Museum of the City of New York, City as Canvas Exhibit. (Indigo)

The Lorraine Hansberry School, IS 167, Bronx, NY. School Yearbook 1991

The Will to Prepare, essay by author   (Postlude)

The Bronx River Project, by student Carol Marie Santiago (Marianna)

How I met a worm face to face, by student Nydia Torres (Marianna)

Personal collection

The Halloween Skate, The author as "A slightly graying Pocahontas," with teacher.   (Chino)

Cast of "The Heart and the Hand are Ready,"one of M. Tanner's original plays.   (Keisha and Malik)

Made in the USA
Columbia, SC
24 September 2017